CHRISTMAS

Vol. 47, No. 8

Publisher, Patricia A. Pingry
Editor, Nancy Skarmeas
Photography and Permissions Editor,
   Kathleen Gilbert
Associate Editor, Fran Morley
Art Director, Patrick McRae
Contributing Editor, Bonnie Aeschliman

ISBN 0-8249-1087-7

IDEALS—Vol. 47, No. 8 December MCMXC IDEALS
(ISSN 0019-137X) is published eight times a year:
February, March, May, June, August, September,
November, December by IDEALS PUBLISHING CORPO-
RATION, P.O. Box 148000, Nashville, Tenn. 37214.
Second-class postage paid at Nashville, Tennessee, and
additional mailing offices. Copyright © MCMXC by IDE-
ALS PUBLISHING CORPORATION. POSTMASTER:
Send address changes to Ideals, Post Office Box 148000,
Nashville, Tenn. 37214-8000. All rights reserved. Title
IDEALS registered U.S. Patent Office.

SINGLE ISSUE—$4.95
ONE-YEAR SUBSCRIPTION—eight consecutive issues as
published—$19.95
TWO-YEAR SUBSCRIPTION—sixteen consecutive issues
as published—$35.95
Outside U.S.A., add $6.00 per subscription year for postage
and handling.

ACKNOWLEDGMENTS

THE APPROACH OF CHRISTMAS from *THE PATH TO
HOME* by Edgar A. Guest. Copyright © 1919 by the Reilly
& Lee Co. All rights reserved. Used by permission of the
Estate; WINTER MORNING from *THE GOLDEN ROAD*
by Edna Jaques. Copyright 1953. Used by permission;
THE CHRISTMAS DAY HEART from *WHITE-CROWN
SINGING* by Dean Collins. Used by permission;
CHRISTMAS IS FOR MEMORIES from *EARTHBOUND
NO LONGER* by Caroline Eyring Miner. Copyright 1961.
Used by permission; THE LASTING GIFTS from
MOMENTS OF SUNSHINE by Garnett Ann Schultz.
Copyright © 1974 by Garnett Ann Schultz. Used by
permission. Our sincere thanks to the following whose
addresses we were unable to locate: Patricia Ann Emme
for A WONDERFUL CHRISTMAS; Helen Monnette for
HELLO, MR. SNOWMAN; Charlotte A. Staak for IT'S
TIME AGAIN FOR CHRISTMAS; Betty Stoffel for THE
RETURNING CHRIST; Mary Stoner Wine for THE ROAD
TO BETHLEHEM; May Gray for THE MEANING.

Four-color separations by Rayson Films, Inc., Waukesha,
Wisconsin

Printing by The Banta Company, Menasha, Wisconsin

The paper used in this publication meets the minimum
requirements of American National Standard for Infor-
mation Sciences—Permanence of Paper for Printed
Library Materials, ANSI Z39.48-1984.

Christmas Cheer

Loy C. Guy

We tramp through the woodland
And gather some pine;
Bring home the holly,
The best of its kind.

Spruce up the parlor,
Garland the door;
Snowflake the pinecones,
Two dozen or more.

Let's frost a window
And frame it with lights;
Sketch in a joy bell
And Santa in flight.

Hark! to the kitchen,
One busy small child
Chops down a stackcake
Ten layers high.

Fling on the glitter
Starlight the tree
While Grandma relaxes
With hot spearmint tea.

Join in the laughter,
Grin ear to ear—
December and Christmas—
The best time of year!

East Haddam, Connecticut
Fred M. Dole Productions

Wonderful Christmas

Patricia Ann Emme

A truly blessed Christmas
Is the gift I'm wishing you.
Filled with joy and laughter,
And with shining dreams come true.

A truly blessed Christmas
That will make the season ring
With all the special magic gifts
That Christmastime can bring!

Christmas Cookies

Eleanor B. Campbell

Star-cut or molded like
  bells in the soft winter breeze;
Some to be tied with a ribbon,
  ready for hanging on Christmas trees;
Or gift-wrapped and sent
to the home of a friend.
How often does love slip unnoticed,
  through doorways on platters and plates?
Home-fashioned offerings waiting on tables
  in kitchens for small celebrations.

Hello, Mr. Snowman!

Helen Monnette

Hello, Mr. Snowman!
You seem so sprite and gay,
Your bright red scarf and mittens
You wear this wintry day;
The buttons black and scarlet,
That tall hat cocked for show,
That cane when you go walking
Your footprints in the snow
Must all delight the children
Who made you in their glee,
Who sing and dance around you
And laugh, delightedly.

Hello, Mr. Snowman!
I beg you not to run,
For your sudden disappearance
Would cancel so much fun.

6

The Candlelight of Christmas

Lee Avery

The candlelight of Christmas
Is glowing through the town,
Not only from house windows
But up the streets and down.

And on the people's faces
A quiet light is seen
From loving and from giving
And faith kept ever green.

There's nothing made of neon
Can make a light as fine
As memory of a blessed Star,
And Christmas candleshine!

It's Time Again for Christmas

It's time again for Christmas
  and the happiness it brings;
It's time again for singing Christmas carols,
  Christmas hymns.
There are loved ones greeting loved ones,
  there's joy in many hearts
There's a nostalgic kind of sadness
  for those who are apart.

It's time again for Christmas
  with its lights and gay array;
It's time for cards and packages,
  time for Santa and his sleigh.
It's time again for Christmas,
  with its gaiety and fun;
Time for saying once again
  "God bless everyone!"

Time to ask for blessing
  for food with love prepared,
And to ask for health and happiness
  throughout the coming year.
Yet Christmas is not just a word
  we use this time of year,
Lest we forget, it means much more,
  open your heart and hear:

Again we tell the story
  of the birthday of a King
Who was born for our redemption,
  whose praises now we sing.
It's time again for Christmas,
  it's time again to say
God bless you now and always
  on this very special day.

Charlotte A. Staak

Reflections

My Thank-You Note

My greatest gift at Christmas
Was not under the Christmas tree,
It had no bows or ribbons,
No shiny paper for all to see.

It came with quiet splendor
On a night so long ago.
Heavenly angels announced the arrival,
Over Bethlehem a star did glow.

Other gifts are lost and forgotten,
Christmas memories fade and die,
But this gift is with me forever,
This gift from God on high.

God's love shone down on Christmas,
From sin He set me free,
Thank you God, for Jesus,
He means so much to me.

Bonnie C. Kane
Gasport, New York

Editor's Note: Readers are invited to submit unpublished, original poetry, short anecdotes, and humorous reflections on life for possible publication in future *Ideals* issues. Please send copies only; manuscripts will not be returned. Writers receive $10 for each published submission. Send material to "Readers' Reflections," Ideals Publishing Corporation, P. O. Box 140300, Nashville, Tennessee, 37214

Winter Morning

Edna Jaques

A morning crisp as watered silk,
   with blankets of new-fallen snow
Tucking the little houses in
   for fear their naked feet will show,
The trees and shrubs are beautiful
   wrapped in their coats of carded wool.

The children on their way to school
   in knitted caps and scarlet coats,
Play hide and seek behind the drifts,
   their laughter rises high and floats
Above the highest maple trees,
   like half-forgotten melodies.

The shop where mother buys the bread
   has glittering panes of frosted glass
Through which the lights take on a glow,
   like holy candles at a mass,
The streets are paved with softest down
   as if a king had come to town.

A sleigh goes by with chiming bells,
   young people riding for a lark,
Their merry voices seem to ring
   with extra sweetness in the dark,
As if they tasted suddenly
   how lovely simple things can be

When Earth puts on her ermine wrap
And holds white diamonds in her lap.

Tamworth, New Hampshire
Dick Smith, Photography

Photo Overleaf
R. Waldkirch/H. Armstrong Roberts, Inc.

Messages

Dorothy Lee

Christmas cards still coming in,
From old friends and from new—
Some are just acquaintances
With special words for you—
From those who gave you happy times,
Their lives were close to yours,
It's fun to greet the mailman
With a pause in household chores.

While winter plays a reckless game
Freezing every town,
The messages on cards become
A warm and welcome gown.
Weather hazards, change of plans?
We slowly move about,
And agree it is a pretty sight
When inside looking out.

So a toast to gay December
As another year soon ends,
Surprises shared in Christmas cards:
Brief moments spent with friends.

Photo Opposite
A Christmas Card Collection
Ina Mackey, Photographer

Colonial Williamsburg—A Step Back in Time

In the restored city of Colonial Williamsburg, Virginia, every aspect of eighteenth-century American life, from the great public events and figures, to the common citizens and the pace of everyday living, is recreated with imagination and precision. The result is an entirely fascinating and complete step back into our nation's beginnings.

The extensive research and archeological expertise behind the restoration of Williamsburg have set the standard for restoration all over the world. Through study of the town's early records and plans, and meticulous attention to detail, the buildings within the historic area have been restored to their original eighteenth-century condition. From the House of Burgesses, where Patrick Henry and Thomas Jefferson shaped our nation's course to democracy, to the Governor's Palace, from which the English Lord Dunmore fled with the rumblings of colonial rebellion in his ears, Williamsburg today is alive with history. There are shops and taverns and restaurants, all maintained and operated much as they were 200 years ago. And it is not only the buildings in Colonial Williamsburg that have been restored; the formal gardens that were a part of most homes in the eighteenth century—a tradition transferred to the colonies from England—have also been carefully recreated.

In Colonial Williamsburg, every effort has also been made to recreate the life and attitudes of the eighteenth century. Visitors can question employees in period costume about antique furniture, silver, paintings, and other collectibles. Demonstrations in area shops give visitors a look at some of the professions of the colonists; blacksmiths, wigmakers, bootmakers, and gunsmiths can all be found on the grounds, with examples of their trade both for sale and for display. Colonial Williamsburg is run—twenty-four hours a day, three-hundred and sixty-five days a year—as a true eighteenth century colonial city, and the guides are well-informed in every detail.

Williamsburg's physical re-creation is astonishingly complete, but what truly sets this city apart from other similar restorations is its desire to provide a comprehensive understanding of the colonial period, beyond the physical artifacts, structures, and costumes. Whereas Williamsburg does concentrate on the large historical events and personalities, it also gives equal attention to those less frequently found in the historical spotlight. There is "The Other Half" tour, which offers a look into the life of Afro-Americans in the colonies, as slaves, and also as free craftsmen and indentured servants. "According to the Ladies" presents another often ignored historical perspective—that of a woman, specifically a

The Colonial Williamsburg Fife and Drums Corps.

female tavern-keeper. Both are wonderful additions to our historical imagination, for while white men dominate the pages of our history textbooks, a knowledge of the roles and attitudes of and about the Afro-Americans and women of the period is needed for a complete cultural picture.

It is hard to categorize the attraction of Williamsburg; this is a complete colonial city. And although Colonial Williamsburg is a major tourist attraction, its founders and management are insistent upon its integrity. The flow of visitors does not disrupt or alter the eighteenth-century mood of the place.

Take a trip to Williamsburg. Walk through its beautiful, quiet streets, where the only traffic is an occasional horse drawn carriage, a team of oxen, or the marching fife and drum corps. Plan several days in the area. Adjacent to the grounds of the restored city is the campus of The College of William and Mary. The second oldest college in the United States, William and Mary is a modern university that remains faithful to its colonial roots. Its well-maintained buildings and grounds complement the architecture and flavor of its historic home city.

Also nearby are Jamestown, the site of America's fist English settlement, and Yorktown, with its battlefield. One hour from either Richmond or Norfolk, Virginia, and only three hours by car from Washington, D.C., Williamsburg and its surrounding region are worth the trip. One can read about colonial America, but Williamsburg offers something beyond facts and dates: a faithful, comprehensive recreation—both in fact and in feeling—of one of America's first cities.

Sheep cross Williamsburg's central green.

An unusual December snow dusts the shops in Merchant's Square.

Christmas in Williamsburg

Colonial Williamsburg is alive with activity throughout the year, but never is the restored city as full of life as during the Christmas season.

The celebration begins with the Grand Illumination, an authentic recreation of an eighteenth-century public Christmas celebration. On an evening in early December, the music of the Fife and Drum Corps leads into the annual display of fireworks, and the city comes to life as a single white candle is illuminated in each window. This is a display of Christmas light unlike anything familiar to most modern eyes, but the effect achieved with simple fireworks and candlelight is as spectacular as any electrically powered celebration. With the Grand Illumination, the streets of Williamsburg are transformed from darkness into a solemn and unforgettable holiday vision, and a season of celebration in true colonial style begins.

The days of the holiday season feature demonstrations and special programs. Visitors can learn to make some of the decorations used in the historic area, all of which are created entirely from natural materials, following the tradition of the early colonists. It was the custom of American colonists to decorate their homes for the holidays with arrangements of pine boughs, nuts, fruits, and dried flowers. Today, in Colonial Williamsburg, these customs are kept intact and an afternoon stroll through the grounds proves that the festive look of Christmas is not completely dependent upon commercial decorations and electric wiring.

TRAVELER'S *Diary*

Residents of the John Blair Kitchen won a blue ribbon in the annual holiday decorating competition among Historic Area residents. More than 500 wreaths of natural materials are displayed throughout Colonial Williamsburg.

Photos courtesy of the Colonial Williamsburg Foundation, Williamsburg, Virginia.

In the evenings Colonial Williamsburg presents eighteenth-century plays and holiday concerts at the Governor's Palace, Bruton Parish Church, and other locations on the grounds, both indoors and out. Winter in Williamsburg is mild, for the most part, and a highlight of the season is the candlelight walking tour through the illuminated colonial capital.

Day or night, Williamsburg at Christmas has a wonderful, festive flavor. The entire community—both resident and visitor—is captivated year after year by the spirit of Christmas the eighteenth century way.

Marian H. Tidwell is a freelance writer in Johnson City, Tennessee.

Shoppers throng the main floor of Macy's in New York.
UPI/Bettman Newsphotos

Forgetting War and Stringing Holly,
U.S. Spends to Make Christmas Jolly

With their peculiar aptitude for invention and escape, Americans prepared for Christmas last week in a manner that reflected no hint of anything but peace, prosperity, and goodwill. The face of the country was bright, busy, and bedecked with the seasonal splendors of stars and holly. Everywhere stores hailed all-time highs in volume of Christmas trade. People were buying enthusiastically, reducing inventories long before schedule. And they were buying big, expensive things like automobiles, refrigerators, radios. Detroit reported that 400,000 new cars had passed from factories to owners in November alone.

But discerning observers noted a mood that contrasted significantly with Christmases of other years. Christmastide of 1940, though gay, bore with it little of the sweet old remembrance of things past, little of the fragrance of evergreens, candles, carols, still snows and silent skies. It brought instead a hectic flush. Streamlined, mass-produced mechanical Santas of identical image grinned and nodded in department store windows from coast to coast. Animate Santa Clauses gagged with girls and airplanes. Decorators did tricks with electricity and plastics. Comic-strip characters and bathing beauties intruded on a show once dominated by the Magi and the Virgin Mary. Phonograph owners flocked to buy a recording of *Silent Night* and *Adeste Fidelis* crooned by Bing Crosby. California vintners reported a boom in domestic wine sales.

And a New York department store which features a $6.95 shirt for Christmas woven of cloth of gold, caused Columnist Lucius Beebe to remark sourly that "the silk-shirts-for working-men era is again at hand."

This strange new 1940 mood was not hard to explain. For a nation that has lived on its nerves for 15 months, the solace and serenity of other seasons was past recall. Only in excitement, in spending, could America forget Coventry, Birmingham and Adolph Hitler. And America had money to spend. Jesse Jones, Secretary of Commerce, announced that factory payrolls were the highest since 1929. Americans were spending because few could foresee any future surety for which to save. And 1940's Christmas was here and now and might at least be merry.

Life, December 23, 1940.

The Christmas Day Heart

Dean Collins

Let me be glad again a little while,
    and see the world all hung with tinsel chains,
Hear reindeer hoofs and see old Santa smile
    through every window's frost-embroidered panes.

Let me unwrap the years and, one by one,
    find each wrapper brighter and more gay,
Till suddenly the gist and goal are won—
    and I unwrap my child's heart stored away.

Let me unwrap the heart that long ago
    beat like a silver bell when morning came,
Hearing the wakened folk move to and fro
    and the big fireplace snap in roaring flame.

Let me unwrap the heart that seemed to climb
    into my throat and throb there mightily
Waiting for father to say: "Now's the time!"
    back flung the doors and bloomed
        the Christmas tree.

Let me unwrap the heart that knew no doubt
    of the great North Pole castle, where all year
Old Santa wrought the toys and trinkets out
    that piled before our raptured vision here.

Let me unwrap the heart that listened well
    to mother singing, and to mother's voice
Tuned with the old reed organ's notes to tell
    how angels came and bade the world rejoice.

Let me unwrap the heart that simply knelt
    with all the rest among the gifts to pray
And stammer out the thanks it truly felt
    unto the One who gave us Christmas Day.

Let me unwrap a heart that leaps in tune
    with that of my own child; a heart that lifts
The same fresh song of joy I hear her croon
    as we kneel, rapt, among our Christmas gifts.

A SLICE OF LIFE

—Edgar A. Guest—

The Approach of Christmas

There's a little chap about our house
    that is being mighty good—
Keeps the front lawn looking tidy
    in the way we've said he should;
Doesn't leave his little wagon,
    when he's finished with his play,
On the sidewalk as he used to;
    now he puts it right away.
When we call him in to supper,
    we don't have to stand and shout;
It is getting on to Christmas
    and it's plain he's found it out.

He eats the food we give him
    without murmur or complaint;
He sits up at the table
    like a cherub or a saint;
He doesn't pinch his sister
    just to hear how loud she'll squeal;
Doesn't ask us to excuse him
    in the middle of a meal,
And at eight o'clock he's willing
    to be tucked away in bed.
It is getting close to Christmas;
    nothing further need be said.

I chuckle every evening
    as I see that little elf,
With the crooked part proclaiming
    that he brushed his hair himself
And I chuckle as I notice
    that his hands and face are clean,
For in him a perfect copy
    of another boy is seen—
A little boy at Christmas
    who was also being good,
Never guessing that his father
    and his mother understood.

There's a little boy at our house
    that is being mighty good;
Doing everything that's proper,
    doing everything he should.
But besides him there's a grown-up
    who has learned life's bitter truth,
Who is gladly living over
    all the joys of vanished youth.
And although he little knows it
    (for it's what I never knew),
There's a mighty happy father
    sitting at the table, too.

Edgar A. Guest began his illustrious career in 1895 at the age of fourteen when his work appeared in the Detroit Free Press. *His column was syndicated in over 300 newspapers, and he became known as "The Poet of the People." Mr. Guest captured the hearts of vast radio audiences with his weekly program, "It Can Be Done" and, until his death in 1959, published many treasured volumes of poetry.*

Christmas Eve 1935

Don Schaubert

The twilight deepened, and smoke struggled to rise through the softly falling snow that spiraled slowly from dark chimneys almost hidden by the white, cottony fluff covering the rooftops. Light, escaping through the stained glass windows of St. Francis Church on the corner of Whitney and Orange Streets, cast colored bands across the snow-covered streets.

Strains of "Silent Night" drifted through the neighborhood from the final rehearsal before Midnight Mass, a Mass that would usher in Christmas 1935 in my hometown of Rochester, New York.

I can still hear that beautiful melody, and fifty-four years later, I can still imagine colored bands of light stretching across the snow-blanketed streets, the snowflakes falling through the light turning all the colors of the rainbow.

I remember how my boots made crunchy

sounding footprints in the new snow. My newspaper deliveries were now almost finished—one more stop, then home for Christmas Eve! How I had looked forward to this day! How different this delivery would be; besides newspapers, I had sixty calendars to present to sixty customers. I hoped they would remember my faithful services and tip generously. It was the depression, and times were tough; any extra money would be needed at home.

My dad, like millions of other unemployed, took those bleak times in stride. Each morning he was up and gone before we five kids came down for breakfast. He might find work for a day or, if lucky, two, maybe three days. Such luck, however, was hard to come by. Still, with Dad's persistence, my three or four dollars a week from the paper route, and Mom's scrimping, we survived. And some generous tips would make our Christmas a little merrier, maybe even put a few more gifts under the tree and a turkey on the table!

The snowfall covered my sled's tracks quickly; the few passersby loomed out of white darkness like huge wound-up toy snowmen. One more delivery!

My mackinaw pockets were heavy with silver coins; there were even two one dollar bills buried among the change. The box on my sled was loaded with presents given to me by customers glad of the service.

In the thirties, it was the custom to give gifts at Christmas to the mailman, the milkman, the garbage man, and of course, the paper boy. These gifts were usually something handmade, something simple—a scarf, a hat, home-baked cookies, nuts, or oranges. I looked forward to sharing these goodies with my brothers and sisters.

Before I was aware of the time passing, I found myself in front of a large gray building. Over a set of massive doors hung a large black sign with gold lettering partially obscured by the accumulated snow. But I knew the sign well: Jacob Straussner Dry Goods. Inside the glass windows that loomed on each side of the doors appeared a veritable treasure-trove of gifts; a feast for the eyes of a young boy intent upon shopping for Christmas.

In the dim light supplied by weak bulbs overhead, I gazed at all the possible gifts for mom and dad, my brothers and sisters. In the left window, I peered at men's dress shirts and ties, sweaters and gloves, shoes and socks. There were women's dresses and aprons and hats. In the right window, a serious-looking teddy bear, sitting next to a child's play set of enameled tin dishes, stared at me. Checker boards, paint sets, tops, harmonicas, and a jacknife competed for my attention; I stared long at the jacknife, for purely for selfish reasons.

Pulling myself away from the windows, I lifted the box cover piled high with snow, and from among my gifts, took out the last paper and calendar. My last delivery: this was the one I had waited for all day.

Now for some serious shopping! I opened the door and the tell-tale bell rang overhead. Mr. Straussner appeared quickly, popping up like one of his jack-in-the-box men. He was small and gnome-like, with large eyes peering out through glasses that sat on unusually large ears. When he smiled, a lone gold tooth shone like a beacon through the gloom of his dimly-lit store. Smiling myself, I wished him a merry Christmas as I handed him his paper and calendar; seconds later, one more dollar bill joined the other two in the depths of my mackinaw.

Excitedly, I prowled the store looking for gifts, Mr. Straussner following close behind. Call it remarkable coincidence, but every gift I purchased seemed to be on sale that afternoon.

With my business completed and another "Merry Christmas" to Mr. Straussner, I opened the massive door and stepped out into the storm. Five more blocks and I would be home. Behind me, in the snow-covered box, were gifts for the entire family, and in my weighted pockets was a special gift for mom and dad, a gift that would ease their worries for a few days.

It was with more than a little pride that I walked into our home on Campbell Street that Christmas Eve, many years ago.

Christmas Queries

Mabel Jones Gabbott

Mother, why do Christmas trees
And Christmas gifts and melodies
Here and all around the earth
Celebrate the Christ child's birth?

Christmas trees are lighted for
The Savior's wondrous brilliant star;
And gifts we give to everyone
Because our father gave His son.

Songs are sung, for on that night
When earth was bathed in holy light
Jesus came—so long ago—
And angels sang to tell us so.

FROM MY G·A·R·D·E·N JOURNAL

Deana Deck

The Christmas Flower

The poinsettia, a traditional symbol of yuletide cheer, comes to us from the pre-Christian, Aztec civilization of Mexico. Considered a symbol of purity, it was a favorite of King Montezuma, and the Aztecs made a rich red dye from its blossoms and used its milky latex sap as a medicine to reduce fevers. The poinsettia was unknown to Europeans until the seventeenth century, when Franciscan priests in Mexico began to incorporate the winter-blooming plant into their nativity processionals during Christmas celebrations.

Its Aztec name is lost to history, but Christian missionaries called poinsettias Flores de Noche

Buena—"flowers of the holy night." This name arose out of the legend of a young peasant girl who gathered up a handful of weeds from along the roadside to bring to her church on Christmas Eve. As she approached the altar, the weeds miraculously bloomed into the brilliant red leaves of the poinsettia. The plant's current name comes from the United States' first minister to Mexico, Joel Roberts Poinsett, who brought the plant to America, where it has become an important part of our holiday traditions.

One aspect of the poinsettia tradition has always been the challenge of nurturing the Christmas poinsettia through the year to see it bloom again the following December. This is a challenge not easily met; the key to success is to lull the plant into thinking it is growing along a road in its arid, subtropical native land instead of in a living room window somewhere in the temperate zone.

The first step is to keep the plant healthy after its holiday debut. Place it in a sunny window and protect it from drafts and sudden temperature changes. By keeping it at a constant 72 degrees in the daytime and about 60 degrees at night, you can prolong the blooming period for several months. Lightly fertilize every three to four weeks.

From spring until mid-summer, give the plant a rest period by gradually decreasing the amount of water you provide. Let the soil dry to the touch between waterings, then flood the pot and discard the drainage. This rest period corresponds to the normal dry spells the poinsettia experiences in the wild. About the first of August, begin to increase waterings and apply fertilizer every two weeks.

As the year draws to a close in the Northern Hemisphere, and days become shorter and nights become longer, artificial light eliminates the effects of seasonal changes on most houseplants. In general, plants thrive with as much light as they can get, and for most, supplemental light in winter is highly beneficial. Not for the photoperiodic poinsettia, however. The plant simply cannot bloom until it receives the shorter-day signal. To help it along, you must provide ten-hour days and fourteen-hour nights from early October into early December, by which time color will be showing.

The colorful petals that are often mistaken for blooms on the poinsettia are actually bracts, or colored leaves, that surround the rather insignificant true flowers, which are yellow and very small. The process that induces the bracts to change from green to red, pink, or white is similar to that which causes color change in autumn leaves.

It is important not to let lamp light or even street lights from a nearby window fall on your poinsettia during its daily darkness cycle. It is equally important to provide it with six or more hours of bright sunlight during the daylight phase. Maintaining this schedule is where many plant owners fail.

Daily routines are not easily altered for the sake of a houseplant. On the other hand, it is very easy to place your poinsettia in a closet or under a box or black plastic trash bag at five o'clock each night and forget to take it out until noon the next day. It is also easy to get distracted at dinnertime and forget to put the plant to bed until seven or eight in the evening. Error in either direction will totally confuse the plant's timing mechanism and it will likely forego blooming altogether.

As yet, I have never had the necessary patience, or time, to follow through completely with the daily closet-to-window routine. I frequently head off in the morning only to remember, halfway through the day, that the poor poinsettia is still languishing under a plastic bag or held captive in a dark closet with only coats and boots for company. Someday, perhaps, when I have more time and fewer distractions, I will win the battle against nature, and I will bring a poinsettia from one Christmas season to the next; but regardless of my success in that area, I will always be sure one way or another to have this beautiful "flower of the holy night" as a part of my own Christmas celebrations.

Deana Deck lives in Nashville, Tennessee, where her garden column is a regular feature in the Tennessean.

POINSETTIAS

J. Harold Gwynne

We hail you, lovely Christmas flower,
   With scarlet petals bright;
How graciously you bear your name:
   "The Flower of Holy Night!"

Your beauty takes the breath away!
   In fields of brilliant blooms;
In gaily planted garden plots;
   In quiet living rooms.

But most of all in every church,
   With chancel all aglow,
You thrill the hearts of worshippers,
   And wondrous beauty show.

You symbolize for all of us
   The hopes of Christmas Day:
You decorate our gifts of love,
   And brighten all our way.

Repeat the message that we need,
   Dear Flower of Holy Night;
Remind us of the savior's love,
   And keep us in His light.

Photo Opposite
Poinsettias
Dick Dietrich Photography

LEGENDARY AMERICANS

Joel Roberts Poinsett

Nancy J. Skarmeas

Most of us go through our lives aspiring to achievement and honor, striving for one goal after another in the hope of leaving our mark, however small or limited, upon the world. It is only human, after all, to desire at least a small taste of immortality.

Joel Roberts Poinsett was no different. Born in 1779 in Charleston, South Carolina, Poinsett devoted his life to public service, moving from one government post to another, always, it would seem, in search of a way to make a contribution to his world and a name for himself in history.

Poinsett was raised in an atmosphere of affluence and intelligence, and he received a thorough education at the country's finest schools. Although his parents envisioned for him a career in law, or perhaps medicine, Poinsett himself was interested in a more immediate and direct sort of service. After leaving law school and touring Europe, he attempted, in 1808, to secure a military appointment in time for the impending war with Great Britain. He was unsuccessful, and he settled, instead, for an appointment as special agent in Chile. There, the energies that Poinsett had hoped to devote to serving his own country were diverted to Chile and its revolution against Spanish rule. Poinsett soon found himself among the leaders of that revolution, and at the heart of a great controversy among Chilean authorities and other foreign representatives stationed in the country. When the revolution failed, Poinsett was forced to return to the United States.

Poinsett's experience in Chile set a pattern for the remainder of his public career. He went on to serve four years in the South Carolina legislature, two years on the South Carolina Board of Public Works, five years as a member of the United States House of Representatives, and four years as the first American minister to Mexico. Poinsett embarked upon each new post with ambition and enthusiasm, but never stuck with any one position long enough to have a serious impact. In the legislature, he remained a relative unknown, never rising beyond the status of junior member, and in Mexico, he failed to gain the acceptance and cooperation of the local government and of the other foreign diplomats stationed there. He left Mexico, much as he had left Chile, at the urging of both the Mexicans and his own government.

After Mexico, Poinsett did achieve a degree of success as Secretary of War under President Van Buren. A lifetime student of military science, Poinsett must have felt that he had finally found his calling, that he had finally come upon the opportunity to make a real and lasting impression on his world. And history proves that such a belief was not entirely unfounded. As far as secretaries of war in Poinsett's era are concerned, he was one of the most successful. He did a great deal to improve military training and education, and he upgraded the status of the mili-

tary in American life.

Yet this is, of course, a small corner of history; a claim to fame, but an obscure one at best. Joel Roberts Poinsett died in 1851, perhaps believing that he had failed in his lifelong quest for achievement and importance. He had known many of the great men and women of his age, and he had served his country devotedly, but he had not set himself apart with any single act or accomplishment that could guarantee his place in history. Or at least he might have believed this to be the case; for if Joel Poinsett did fail, it was in not recognizing his most lasting and wonderful achievement.

Besides being a diplomat and statesman, in his time away from the rush of appointments and elections, Poinsett was an avid amateur botanist. While in Mexico, during what was probably the most frustrating point in his professional career, Poinsett often sought relaxation in his gardens. When he returned to the United States, he brought back with him a favorite plant from these gardens, a beautiful specimen of subtropical plant of the euphorbia family, a plant with brilliant red leaves unlike anything seen before in the United States. Back in Charleston, retired for a time from public life, Poinsett cultivated his Mexican plant, which was eventually named poinsettia in is honor.

And it is this flower—our Christmas flower—that carries the name of Joel Roberts Poinsett through the pages of history. It is ironic that this man, so obsessed with war and politics, should owe his fame to a single plant, a beautiful, unusual flower that makes only a brief appearance in American life each December. With its combination of red and green and white, the poinsettia has become an instant symbol of our Christmas celebrations—both of the festive colors and the solemn beauty of the season. Today, the name of the man who wanted to fight wars and win fame in the service of his country lives on in the name of the plant that symbolizes joy and peace each Christmastime, a reminder that we can't always understand the meaning and the significance of our lives, and that often, honor and accomplishment and service arise out of our simplest, most private pursuits.

A GIFT FROM YOUR KITCHEN

A gift from your kitchen is a gift from your heart. Jars of colorful Raisin Winter Fruit Relish—a confetti combination of raisins, fresh fruit, and red bell pepper—take only ten minutes to make. Sweet and tangy, our relish is a delightful accompaniment to typical holiday fare such as ham, turkey, or other roasted meats. This makes it an especially welcome gift for the season, and also a wonderful addition to your own table!

RAISIN WINTER FRUIT RELISH

2   cups distilled white vinegar
2   cups sugar
4   cups natural and/or golden raisins
$1/3$ cup coarsely chopped candied ginger or 2 tablespoons mustard seeds
1   teaspoon red pepper flakes
4   cups peeled, cored, and diced firm pears or tart apples
1   cup diced red bell pepper

Mix vinegar and sugar in Dutch oven. Add raisins, ginger, and pepper flakes. Bring to a boil. Reduce heat; simmer five minutes. Mix in pears and bell pepper. Return to a boil. Simmer five minutes. Spoon into jars; cool. Store in refrigerator.* Drain and serve with meats, poultry, and cheeses. Makes about eight cups.

*Relish will keep in refrigerator for about one month. Instead of refrigerating, relish may be processed in hot water bath according to canning jar manufacturer's instructions. Allow ten minutes for half-pint jars, fifteen minutes for pints.

Bonnie Aeschliman is a teacher of occupational home economics and a freelance food consultant. She lives in Wichita, Kansas, with her husband and their two children.

COLLECTOR'S CORNER

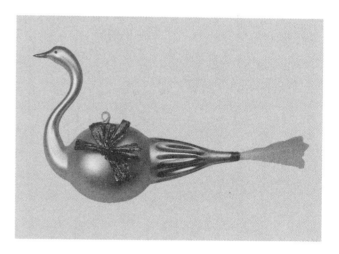

Glass Christmas Tree Ornaments

Christmas trees were first decorated in Germany in the late 1500s. The evergreen Christmas tree symbolized eternal life, and the decorations consisted of apples to signify man's fall from grace and white communion wafers to represent his salvation. Our traditional Christmas colors originated from this combination of red, white, and green.

As time passed, other fruits, and even vegetables, were added, along with small candles and a star on the top to welcome the Christ child. The decorations on the tree, from their inception until the late 1800s, were primarily used as gifts.

The decorated Christmas tree's popularity spread rapidly from Germany throughout northern Europe in the mid-1800s. And as America was settled, each immigrant brought to the new country holiday customs from his or her homeland. Although American Christmas traditions do go back to the founding of our country, it was not until the 1890s that Christmas became a legal holiday in all states, and it was not until the influx of diverse immigrant groups in the nineteenth century that American Christmas as we know it today came to exist.

The Germans not only originated the Christmas tree, but led in the manufacture of decorations, too. Blown glass ornaments were the first commercial tree decorations. They are also the first type of Christmas ornament to become a collectible.

The town of Lauscha, in the Thuringian Mountains of East Germany, has been known for its glassmaking for centuries. Originally, glass beads were the main product, although they also made kugels—large decorative glass ball ornaments. Kugels were placed in windows or, because they were too heavy for a tree, suspended from the ceiling. When foreign competition hurt the glass bead business, the idea of selling Christmas tree decorations took root, and a booming business was begun.

Even as late as 1921, the ornament business in Lauscha was carried out much as it was in the 1800s: as a non-mechanized family enterprise. First, the ornaments were handblown, coated inside with a silvery solution, colored, lacquered, and then given detail and hangers. With each member assigned a specific job, an industrious family could make about six hundred ornaments in a single day.

soon followed suit, and by the mid-1930s, more than 250 million glass ornaments were being imported each year. Most of these were made in molds, although some were freeblown.

German glass ornaments proved to be so popular that other countries were soon producing their own. However, for the most part, these efforts produced an inferior product, and Germany continued to dominate the industry.

When looking for antique glass ornaments, the most important variable is the condition. Check the paint for cracks and chipping. Although age is important, subject matter or country of origin are often more crucial in determining the ornament's value. A collector should inspect the ornament's neck first; a narrow neck is indicative of German manufacture, and thus, for the most part, better quality.

The relative age of an ornament can often be determined by the hanger. The first hangers were made of cork, and later, brass clips were used. Between 1900 and 1910, both dull gray caps and brass caps were made with small openings for wire, and after 1910 a spring-hook hanger was the standard.

Among the collectible glass ornaments, there are more than five thousand different designs. Favorites are grape clusters, pickles, ears of corn, Santas, clowns, houses, churches, umbrellas,

The ornaments in these photographs are from the personal collection of Virginia Stovall, Nashville, Tennessee

Glass ornaments reached America in the 1860s through German immigrants. It was an American, however, F.W. Woolworth, who started the glass ornament craze in the United States.

In 1880, Woolworth owned a single store in Lancaster, Pennsylvania. Although he was skeptical of their success, he bought a few glass ornaments to sell. They became an immediate hit, and within ten years, Woolworth was importing the ornaments directly from Germany for his growing chain of stores. Other American companies

birds, fish, cats, and bears. Enthusiastic collectors sometimes keep Christmas trees up year round to display their prized ornaments.

Christmas is a holiday rich in history and significance. Glass ornaments provide an ideal Christmas collectible—symbolizing not only the traditions and people of the past, but representing the fragility of those memories, and of life itself.

Carol Shaw Johnston, a public school teacher, writes articles and short stories. She lives with her family in Brentwood, Tennessee.

CRAFTWORKS

Painted Holiday Sweatshirts

These painted sweatshirts, designed by Mary Beaty, are simple to make with materials found at any craft store. The key to the sweatshirts is your own creativity—Mary provides the basic instructions, but you will need to supply the rest. With a little imagination and experimentation, these personalized, painted sweatshirts make the perfect holiday gift for friends and family.

Materials:

One plain-colored sweatshirt
Print fabric
Fabric adhesive
Silver and/or gold acrylic glitter paint
White puff paint (acrylic)
Natural bristle paint brushes (small, medium, and large size)

Step One:

Choose a piece of print fabric with a design appropriate for cutting. Most fabric stores have a selection of print material. All you need is one complete design that will fit on the front of your shirt. The sweatshirt pictured features a row of Christmas shops, but the specific design is up to you—Santas, Christmas trees, snow scenes, packages, or decorations all work well. Once you have chosen the fabric, cut carefully around the edges of the selected design. Cut as close to the edge as possible, but don't worry about slight imperfections; the design will eventually be outlined in puff paint.

Step Two:

Cut a section of fabric adhesive to the exact size of your fabric piece. Iron the fabric to your sweatshirt according to the directions on the fabric adhesive package. Once again, the exact placement of the fabric on the sweatshirt is up to you. Experiment with different placements before using adhesive.

Step Three:

Highlight your fabric design with silver and/or gold glitter paint. Use the glitter to add light and accent. The three brush sizes will allow you to achieve a variety of effects.

Step Four:

Use the white puff paint to outline your design and add detail, following the directions for use on the paint container. White puff paint is perfect for Christmas designs because when dry and puffed, it will look just like snow. Allow the puff paint to dry flat for twenty-four hours. Then turn the sweatshirt inside out. With a piece of brown paper between the iron and the sweatshirt, lightly steam the back of the painted area (approximately 30 seconds). This will cause the paint to puff.

Care Instructions:

These painted sweatshirts can be hand washed with mild soap without causing damage to the paint. Make sure that your paints are all acrylic, and that you pay attention to the care instructions on your sweatshirt. With a little extra care, your sweatshirt will last through years of Christmases.

Mary Beaty is cosmetologist who, in her spare time, works on painting and other crafts. In addition to her sweatshirts, she designs wedding gowns and wedding cakes, makes her own jewelry, and does floral arrangements. She lives in Brentwood, Tennessee, with her husband and their two children.

Photo by Gerald Koser

THROUGH MY WINDOW

Pamela Kennedy

The Other Mother at the Manger

Miriam! Hurry, the guests need their breakfast! Miriam!"

The irritated and urgent voice of her husband broke through Miriam's daydreams and she swiftly refolded the tiny gown she had been holding, tucking it hastily back into the acacia trunk.

"Coming Benjamin!" she called. Quickly smoothing a few errant strands of hair back under her scarf and lifting her long skirts, she dashed down the steps to the large eating room below. She spied her husband with his arms folded, a scowl on his face as he listened to a complaining customer. Ducking into the kitchen, Miriam soon had the serving girls dashing about with trays of fruit and oat cakes, waiting upon the hungry men with efficiency.

"Miriam!" She started at her name and spun around to face Benjamin. He towered over her, his dark hair and eyebrows glinting in the early morning sun that streamed into the small kitchen. He was a handsome man with smooth, olive skin and bright, dark eyes. His attractiveness was marred only by the scowl he habitually wore these days. Miriam suspected it was because of

her, and the blame wore heavily on her heart.

"Yes, Benjamin?" Her eyes searched his for the hint of tenderness she used to see there.

"This is the time of the census," he scolded. "You cannot be lolling in bed when the inn is filled with guests who need to be cared for. We cannot expect to keep their business if we do not serve them well."

A caustic retort hovered behind Miriam's lip, but she swallowed it like a hard lump of dough and only nodded.

Apparently satisfied, Benjamin turned and left the kitchen. Angrily, Miriam stoked the fire in the small oven, sending sparks and ashes falling in the morning breeze. "Lolling in bed," she muttered as she banged crockery and emptied dirty plates and goblets. Suddenly, like an uncontrollable wave within her, a great sob welled up and she ran from the kitchen into the tiny garden behind the house. There, she fell on her knees beneath the solitary olive tree and wept.

Behind her, in silence, Benjamin stood and watched. The dark scowl was gone and tenderness filled his deep-set eyes. But he did not go to Miriam. He was afraid; afraid she blamed him

46

and would never forgive him, afraid they could never recapture their love and joy now that the baby was gone. And so he left her alone with her grief and tied his own in an angry knot within himself.

Her despair spent, Miriam leaned against the narrow trunk of the tree and breathed deeply of the morning scents. Small birds skipped among the tree tops and chirped to one another, quarreling over a bit of berry or a leaf.

"How does the world continue as if nothing has happened?" she wondered. The Bethlehem sky was still a bright azure blue, the birds and insects still labored, the wind still blew, the flowers continued to bloom. Only her child, her tiny son, was no more.

A quarrel from the kitchen interrupted her thoughts and she hurried back inside to see what was the matter. After settling the dispute between two jealous serving girls, Miriam saw to the cleaning of the dining room and supervised the dusting and sweeping out of the rooms of the inn. The day passed quickly, one demand following upon the heels of another, and it was soon time to prepare the evening meal.

Caesar's census, although generating much displeasure among the populace, certainly kept the innkeeper busy. The previous months had been lean, and Miriam was pleased that though the work was hard, they would experience some security as a result of it.

The sun had set and the early evening sky was punctuated with glimmering stars. Miriam overheard Benjamin's voice as she entered the dining room. "No, I am sorry, we are filled. We have no more room." She walked to his side and spoke as he shut the heavy wooden door.

"How many have you turned away?" she asked.

"At least a dozen," he answered. "It's a pity we haven't more space. I could fill every room and turn a good profit." He looked into her dark eyes for a moment, then smiled. "And you could buy those silver bracelets you have been eyeing at old Pasha's stall in the market!"

Miriam blushed at his teasing words and returned his smile with a timid one of her own.

Apparently awkward with even this small exchange of emotion, Benjamin cleared his throat and surveyed his guests as they dined. "They seem to be enjoying your meal tonight," he declared without even looking at Miriam.

She nodded. "Lamb is always popular," she replied, wishing she could say something to recapture the fragile moment they had just shared. "Have you eaten, Benjamin? Perhaps I could bring you a plate . . ."

Her suggestion was interrupted by a loud banging on the door. Benjamin turned and pulled it open, revealing a tired and dusty man. Before the fellow could speak, Benjamin told him the inn was full.

Miriam watched as the hopeful expression faded on the weary face. "Isn't there anywhere you could put us? My wife is with child and her time is near. We have come all the way from Nazareth."

"Joseph. Oh, Joseph."

Miriam recognized the urgency and anguish of the woman's cry and pushed past Benjamin and around the man outside. She reached up and lifted the young woman from the back of the tired little donkey. Her own recent pregnancy caused Miriam to feel an immediate bond with the poor girl.

"Benjamin," she insisted with a rare forcefulness, "we must take them in. The girl is in labor!"

Benjamin glowered at his wife. He didn't want a stranger to hear her talk to him in such a way and he didn't want anything to do with another woman in labor. "There is no room!" he repeated, folding his arms over his chest with finality.

"Then make room!" Miriam snapped at him.

Benjamin's eyes blazed with fury and his face reddened at her insolence. "There is no room!" he cried once more and slammed the heavy door.

Joseph turned with embarrassment and began to apologize to Miriam, but she waved off his words with a gesture of impatience. "Don't worry, it will be all right." Her mind raced as she tried to think of a solution. The girl groaned again and Joseph picked her up, holding her in his arms, calming her with soft assurances.

"Come," Miriam commanded as she grabbed the lead on the donkey. She guided the couple around the inn to the stable behind. After tethering the animal, Miriam cleared out a small area behind the sheep's pen. Wielding an old straw broom, she vigorously swept out the dust and stones, disturbing several roosting hens and dozing sheep. Having cleared the stony floor, she grabbed large armfuls of sweet hay and arranged a deep, soft bed. Unfastening her shawl, she spread it across the hay and then turned to Joseph. "Put her down here," she directed. "It's not fancy, but it is clean and will be quiet. Loosen her robes and make her comfortable. I need to get a few things."

As Joseph placed his wife upon the hay, Miriam caught a glimpse of her face. It was pale and oval, framed by dark auburn hair. Her skin had the dewey freshness of youth, but in her eyes shone an ageless serenity.

"What is your name?" Miriam asked softly as she prepared to go.

"Mary," the young woman answered.

"Well, Mary," Miriam continued with a smile of assurance, "I think you will be a mother by morning! Now you lie here and count the stars until I return. It will help pass the time."

Avoiding the dining area and the chance of an encounter with her husband, Miriam dashed up the back stairway and into their room. She threw open the small acacia chest and felt a sharp tightening in her heart. Forcing herself to reach inside, she removed the small garments she had so lovingly and tearfully stored there only weeks ago. Sorting quickly, she decided upon two wrapping cloths of fine wool and a pure white linen gown embroidered in pale yellow. Grabbing a stack of towels and a basin for water, Miriam ran back down the stairway and out to the stable.

Joseph knelt beside Mary, holding her hand and speaking to her softly. Miriam watched them for a moment, envying the love they shared. Then she spoke quietly.

"Joseph, would you fill this with water from the jar beside the kitchen door? I'll tend to Mary." Miriam sat beside the laboring woman and helped her through the ever-stronger contractions. When Joseph returned with the water, she dipped a towel into the basin and cooled Mary's brow and bathed her dusty arms and feet.

Throughout the night the two women worked together, and as they did each spoke of her dreams and longings. Bound together by the common experience of bringing forth life, they were no longer strangers.

When at last the tiny newborn came, he was perfect and strong. Quickly, Miriam wrapped him in the soft, swaddling clothes she had so lovingly prepared for her own son. Then she laid him gently in his mother's arms and felt the emptiness in her own.

Mary gazed into her baby's eyes—the eyes so filled with the promise of eternity. Then she glanced at Miriam and saw the longing there. "Would you like to hold him?" she offered.

Miriam hesitated before holding out her arms to take the child. Instead of feeling the pain of loneliness, she knew a flood of peace as she looked upon the babe. Something deep within her was released and a new hope took its place. "What will you call him?" she whispered.

"His name is Jesus," Mary replied, "for he is the Father's promise now fulfilled."

Miriam shifted slightly and the light from a single brilliant star illuminated the tiny sleeping face. "Jesus," she said. "Welcome, little Jesus. Welcome to the world."

A soft cough broke the stillness and Miriam turned quickly, catching sight of Benjamin walking slowly away from the stables. His shoulders were stooped and his steps weary. Miriam looked once more at the baby Jesus, tenderly kissed his flawless cheek, then gently returned him to his mother. "I must go," she whispered.

Noiselessly, Miriam caught up with her husband and pulled at his sleeve to stop him. As he looked at her, she saw the shimmer of tears reflected in the light from the star above. There were no words, but none were needed. She slipped her hand into his and as they walked up the narrow stairway together, Miriam knew something more than a baby had been born that night.

Pamela Kennedy is a freelance writer of short stories, articles, essays, and children's books. Married to a naval officer and mother of three children, she has made her home on both U.S. coasts and currently resides in Hawaii. She draws her material from her own experiences and memories, adding bits of imagination to create a story or mood.

The Returning Christ

Betty W. Stoffel

At Christmastime when every heart
  with special rapture fills,
Each soul becomes a Bethlehem
  among Judean hills,

And Jesus Christ, the Son of God,
  in His own lowly way
Comes seeking room in human hearts
  to share the Christmas Day.

May He not find the crowded inn
  too full for Him again,
Or Christmas gifts and Christmas trees
  without the Christ of men.

But may there be the humble heart
  with room prepared and blessed,
And heart reborn to greet anew
  the long-expected guest.

At Christmas when He seeks His place
  supreme in human wills,
Each heart becomes a Bethlehem
  among Judean hills.

The Road to Bethlehem

Mary Stoner Wine

If we have knelt confessing
     all our sin and wrong,
If we've received forgiving grace
     and found a song,
Then we may follow heaven's star
     to Bethlehem,
And we may crown our Lord
     with love's rich diadem.

If we have conquered selfish pride,
     then we may know
God's peace, and join the angels' praise
     with hearts aglow.
If through our lives, God's love
     flows out to men,
We too have found the Star,
     the road to Bethlehem.

And so it came to pass in those days, that there went out a decree from Ceasar Augustus, that all the world should be taxed. And this taxing was first made when Cyrenius was governor of Syria. And all went to be taxed, every one into his own city.

And Joseph also went up from Galilee, out of the city of Nazareth, into Judea, unto the city of David, which is called Bethlehem; because he was of the house and lineage of David, to be taxed with Mary his espoused wife, being great with child.

And so it was, that while they were there, the days were accomplished that she should be delivered.

And she brought forth her firstborn son, and wrapped him in swaddling clothes, and laid him in a manger; because there was no room for them in the inn.

Luke 2: 1-7

Christmas Star

Jane K. Nutt

A diamond shines no brighter
    than that lovely Christmas star.
It shines in all its brilliance;
    it's seen from near or far.
A symbol of the Christ child
    as He lay upon the hay,
It tells to all the waiting world
    a King was born that day.

O Bethlehem Star keep shining—
    give us faith and hope and love.
Keep our thoughts forever turning
    to the Savior up above.
Give us strength and hope and courage
    to do our best by far
And never falter in our faith
    as we watch that Christmas star!

Guiding Light

Wanda M. Trawick

When they followed
   that light from afar,
    did it twinkle—
      that Christmas star?
Did it wink and blink
   in the black of the night,
    or did it glow
      with a steady light?
As they rode the camels,
   were their faces turned
    toward the evening sky
      where the bright star burned?
And are my eyes fixed
   upon that light
    that would guide me
      through my own dark night?

And there were in that same country, shepherds abiding in the field, keeping watch over their flock by night.

And, lo, the angel of the Lord came upon them, and the glory of the Lord shone round about them: and they were sore afraid.

And the angel said unto them, Fear not; for, behold, I bring you good tidings of great joy, which shall be to all people. For unto you is born this day in the city of David a Saviour, which is Christ the Lord.

And this shall be a sign unto you; ye shall find the babe wrapped in swaddling clothes, lying in a manger.

And suddenly there was with the angel a multitude of the heavenly host praising God, and saying, Glory to God in the highest, and on earth peace, good will toward men.

Luke 2: 8-14

The Meaning

May Gray

You ask
The meaning of Christmas.
Christmas is many things:
A star in the sky;
A song on lifted wings.
Christmas is a landscape;
Wonder in the face
Of a little child,
A birthday and a place.

And Christmas is a mother
Shawled against the night
Under a lowly roof,
Beneath a flaming light,
Pondering in her heart
How it could be
Her arms held God's love
For all humanity.

A Candle Burned

Eliza Britt Ray

A candle burned in Bethlehem,
Within a stable bare.
It shone upon the cattle, and
Upon the Christ child fair.
It made a glow upon the walls;
It brightened Mary's face.
It hallowed every corner of
That crude and humble place.

A candle burns within my heart.
Oh let me guard the flame,
That seeing it, the world may know
Devotion to his name.
Oh may its light burn warm and true,
Its glow so constant be,
That other candles will be lit
In other hearts for Thee.

Now when Jesus was born in Bethlehem of Judea in the days of Herod the king, behold, there came wise men from the east to Jerusalem. Saying, where is he that is born King of the Jews? For we have seen his star in the east, and are come to worship him.

Matthew 2:1-2

Then Herod, when he had privily called the wise men, enquired of them diligently what time the star appeared. And he sent them to Bethlehem, and said, Go and search diligently for the young child; and when ye have found him, bring me word again, that I may come and worship him also.

When they had heard the king, they departed; and lo, the star, which they saw in the east, went before them, till it came and stood over where the young child was. When they saw the star, they rejoiced with exceeding great joy.

And when they were come into the house, they saw the young child with Mary his mother, and fell down, and worshiped him; and when they had opened their treasures, they presented unto him gifts; gold, and frankincense, and myrrh. And being warned of God that they should not return to Herod, they departed into their own country another way.

Matthew 2:7-12

Frankincense
and Myrrh
and Gold

Ethel Dietrich

The tree is trimmed, the stockings hung,
The stories read, the carols sung,
Gifts are waiting beneath the tree,
Stockings bulging with mystery.

The scene is set for Christmas night
But then, before I dim the light,
There in the stable small and brown
I lay the baby Jesus down

Gently in his manger bed,
Wispy hay to pillow his head—
"Welcome, welcome, little one,
Child of Mary, God's own Son."

Somehow I feel the hours spent
In making Christmas evident—
The wrappings sparkling green and red,
The sugar cakes and gingerbread,

Beribboned wreaths and candleshine—
These are proferred gifts of mine
Made of love and thought and time,
Just little gestures, nothing fine,

Still, offered in his name today,
My efforts seem in some small way
Much like the Magi's gifts of old—
My frankincense and myrrh and gold.

The Lasting Gifts

Garnett Ann Schultz

So many times dear ones shall ask
What would you like this day,
And what would bring you Christmas joy
That I might give away,
A question posed a hundred times
And yet we do forget,
The treasures that would mean the most
The dearest gifts to get.

Expectancy—rich happiness
Good health that means so much,
Undying faith in God above
A loved one's tender touch,
A peace of mind—a happy heart
A confidence serene,
A worthwhile thought to live and grow
A lovely lasting dream.

These are the gifts—the lasting gifts
To treasure through the years,
A zest for living each new day
A smile instead of fears,
What would you like this Christmas Day
So much we all possess,
Abundantly our God gives all
In lasting happiness.

Photo Opposite
South Stratford, Vermont
Fred M. Dole Productions

Country
CHRONICLE
—————— Lansing Christman ——————

Lucile and I were privileged to share fifty-seven Christmastimes together. This is the second Christmas I have been alone. But she is in my heart and in my memories, memories of the richest kind.

Going through her keepsakes, I came upon a poem I had written for her one past Christmas:

These are the hours of Christmastime.
I watch a gentle form working the swaying
    boughs of the evergreen.

Her hands and fingers place the strings of
    colored lights on the limbs that bend and
        stir as if she were a soft wind,
As if the lights were the stars, or perhaps the
    glittering colors that show when a thin
        cloud sails under the glow of the moon.
Hers is a magic hand, and the heart of love
    pouring gladness into other hearts, and in
        her own heart, and mine.
Her hair is the moon brushing gently across
    the hemlock hill, spreading shadows and

friendliness over December fields.
She is the night—resting her soft golden head
on the pure white pillows of snow.

Lucile and I concluded a long time ago that the true meaning of Christmas is love and companionship and faith in God. It is, I think, that faith and love that give me strength to endure. I know that Lucile is at home and at peace with God; that gives me comfort.

When I look up at the stars in the heavens, I think of Christmas and the star in the East. I think of the birth of Jesus Christ, our Lord. And because of that night in Bethlehem nearly 2,000 years ago, Christmas shines with the glory of God, promising everlasting life.

These two yuletides later, though I need time to grieve, I feel the joyous spirit of Christmas. So let the bells ring! Let the hymns and carols pour forth from your hearts! I wish you love and peace and joy this Christmastime!

The author of two published books, Lansing Christman has been contributing to Ideals _for almost twenty years. Mr. Christman has also been published in several American, foreign, and braille anthologies. He lives in rural South Carolina._

hank you, God, for sending Jesus down to earth. So he could tell us all about you and show us how to live.

He was the very best Christmas present we ever got.

For God so loved the world that He gave His one and only son.

John 3:16

Christmas Returns

Paul Swope

Busy, bustling, happy season
Pushing madly through the throngs
For that single, special present
In the background, Christmas sounds;

Nerves are frayed and tempers edgy,
Lists are long and time is fleeting,
But we turn aside our anger
With a happy "Season's Greeting."

Friends and strangers share the feeling
Peace and goodwill everywhere—
Christmas Day is now upon us,
We join with those for whom we care.

Then the season's magic passes
And the shops are full once more,
Things don't fit and some seem garish,
So we return them to the store.

Clerks are snappish, ugly feeling,
Hustling, jostling in the crowd;
Things are getting back to normal
Hostile feelings, comments loud . . .

If we only had "Exchange Desks"
Where someone with kindly cheer
Would "return" our Christmas spirit
For our use throughout the year!

A Special Time

Judy Schwab

Shopping lists,
    kitchen smells,
Children singing,
    Jingle Bells—
Colored lights,
    falling snow,
Fireplace,
    with amber glow—
Trees adorned,
    a holly bough,
Parties, friends,
    blessings now—

Memories shared,
    a quiet tear,
Some are gone,
    still wanted here—
A time of Peace,
    and hope renewed,
Our fellow man,
    with love imbued—
A host of things,
    so many more,
To answer then,
    what's Christmas for?

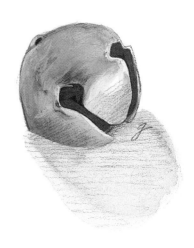

Photo Opposite
Christmas Tree with Antique Ornaments
Larry Lefever/Grant Heilman Photography

BITS & PIECES

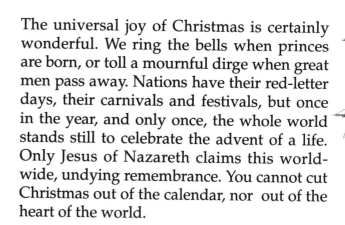

Blow, bugles of battle, the marches of peace;
East, west, north, and south let the long
    quarrel cease;
Sing the song of great joy that the angels
    began,
Sing the glory to God and of good-will
    to man!

John Greenleaf Whittier

The universal joy of Christmas is certainly wonderful. We ring the bells when princes are born, or toll a mournful dirge when great men pass away. Nations have their red-letter days, their carnivals and festivals, but once in the year, and only once, the whole world stands still to celebrate the advent of a life. Only Jesus of Nazareth claims this world-wide, undying remembrance. You cannot cut Christmas out of the calendar, nor out of the heart of the world.

Author Unknown

It is the most human and kindly of seasons, as fully penetrated and irradiated with the feeling of human brotherhood, which is the essential spirit of Christianity, as the month of June with sunshine and the balmy breath of roses.

George W. Curtis

We therefore welcome our Christmas in December. The "worship of Christ" could not have a better setting than amid the domestic festivities, social forces, and generous and man-helping deeds of our Christmas-tide. In no more fitting way can we say good-bye to the closing year; and All hail! to the new.

John Clifford

75

Photo Overleaf
St. Joseph's Catholic Basilica
Milwaukee, Wisconsin
Henry J. Hupp/Laatsch-Hupp Photo

Christmas Is for Memories

Caroline Eyring Miner

Father performed the ritual of the fire—
A mighty log was placed upon the hearth,
And as the crackling flames ascended higher,
We felt there was no sweeter sound on earth!
The day before we'd climbed for mistletoe
And dragged the clustered greens with berries white
Into the living room, and to and fro
We'd moved the Christmas tree till it was right;
Then deluged it with icicles made of tin,
With paper chains and egg-white popcorn strings.
Frost pictures on the windows made with thin
Soap lines revealed the magic winter brings.
Our humble home became a spangled hall,
For love and gentleness encircled all.

Christmas is made of memories replete—
The footfall of imagined reindeer swift
As birds in flight, the cheery faces you meet
In passing on the street of one with gift
Wrapped well with ribbon bows of red and green,
With love tucked deftly in; the wistful face
Of small boy pressed against a window seen
To hold the wished-for glamorous gear to grace
A hero of the diamond; the sharp smell
Of evergreen, and spicy wassail cup;
Bright candies heaped so temptingly they spell
Your downfall pound by pound. You note that up
Beside the mantle clock red candles glow,
So bit by bit your happy memories grow.

They're gone, who made my Christmas memories,
Placed mirrors in my life to catch the glow
All down the years. I wish that they could know
How much the little things they did have played
Sweet music in my ears. The melodies
Sung around the old piano still will go
With me through every Christmas, even grow
More tender; little gifts of love they made
Were priceless. As we decorate our tree
And light our fire on the hearth tonight,
And place the candles so that all may see,
And sing old songs, our children find delight;
They build their dreams, and in this Christmas chain
Of memories repeat the glad refrain.

Readers' Forum

I saw my first Ideals *magazine in a thrift shop, since then, I won't let my subscription run out. I love everything about the magazine, the pictures, the poems. I read it to the grandchildren. I love the craftworks, from the sunbonnet pillow I made a quilt for my granddaughter and next will make a pillow and quilt from neckties for the grandsons.*

I truly enjoy your great magazine.

Helen Morrissey
Antigo, Wisconsin

I have been a subscriber to Ideals *for some time now, and would like to say that the last issue known as* Ideals *Country is in a class by itself. I am an old timer, all of 79 years of age, so I came up from horse and buggy days. Those peaceful country scenes really hit the spot with me . . . I find your magazine so refreshing after what you see nowadays. Be sure that I will continue my subscription when it is due. I used to be a sign painter, when I retired, I began to do a lot of landscape art in oils . . . Your magazine gives me many ideas and much inspiration.*

Jens Rasmussen
Siren, Wisconsin

Want to share your crafts?
Readers are invited to submit original craft ideas for possible development and publication in future Ideals *issues. Please send query letter (with photograph, if possible) to Editorial Features Department, Ideals Publishing Corporation, P.O. Box 140300, Nashville, Tennessee 37214-0300. Please do not send craft samples; they cannot be returned.*

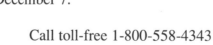